WRESTLING
CITY AUDITORIUM
FRI. MAY 10
Return Championship Match
DICKIE
STEINBORN
VS
TARZAN TYLER
NO TIME LIMIT
JOHN CENA
SUMMER
SLAM
PER-VIEW
SANDCASTLE
BLACKPOOL
EVERY SUNDAY NIGHT
FROM 5th JULY
TOP U.K. & WORLD STARS IN ACTION including
BIG DADDY
in a SUPER SIZE TAG CLASH
GIANT
HAYSTACKS
Marty JONES
ALAN KILBY
KANGAROOS
McGREGOR
McDONALD
SAMSON
THE LEGENDARY
KENDO
NAGASAKI
RONNIE ETCHISON
PEDRO ZAPATA
CHRIS
BELKAS
LEGENDS
OF
WRESTLING

I0902083

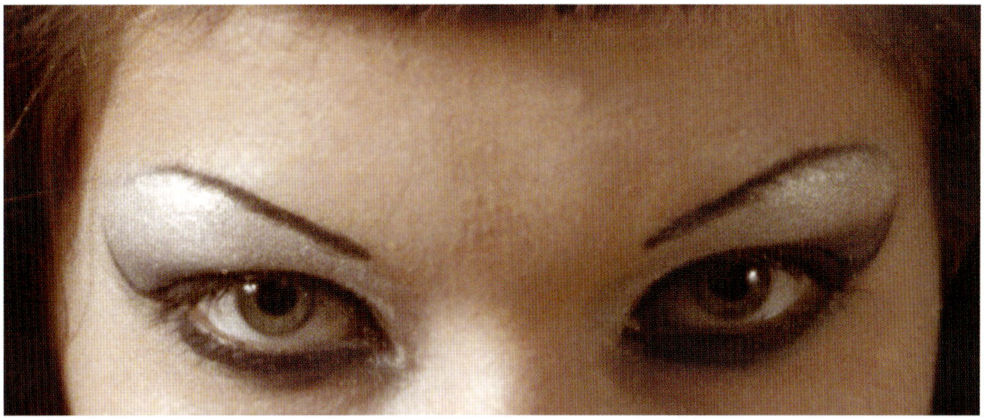

HARD BOYS + BAD GIRLS

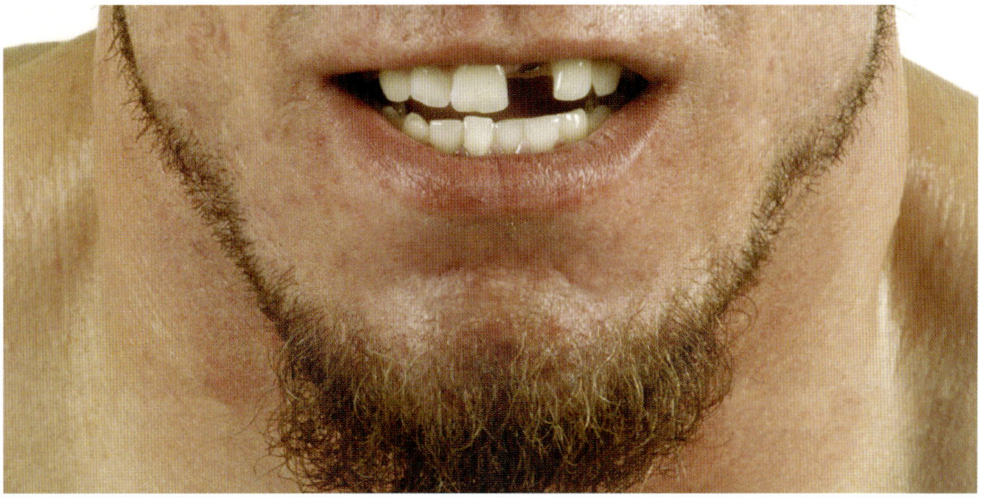

Thomas McGovern

Schiffer Publishing Ltd
4880 Lower Valley Road · Atglen, Pennsylvania 19310

Schiffer Books are available at special discounts for b[illegible] purchases for sales promotions or premiums. Spec[illegible] editions, including personalized covers, corporate imprin[illegible] and excerpts can be created in large quantities for spec[illegible] needs. For more information contact the publishe[illegible]

Published by Schiffer Publishing Ltd.
4880 Lower Valley Road
Atglen, PA 19310
Phone: (610) 593-1777; Fax: (610) 593-2002
E-mail: Info@schifferbooks.com

For the largest selection of fine reference books on this and related subjects, please visit our web site at **www.schifferbooks.com** We are always looking for people to write books on new and related subjects. If you have an idea for a book please contact us at the above address.

This book may be purchased from the publisher.
Include $5.00 for shipping.
Please try your bookstore first.
You may write for a free catalog.

In Europe, Schiffer books are distributed by
Bushwood Books
6 Marksbury Ave.
Kew Gardens
Surrey TW9 4JF England
Phone: 44 (0) 20 8392 8585; Fax: 44 (0) 20 8392 9876
E-mail: info@bushwoodbooks.co.uk
Website: www.bushwoodbooks.co.uk

Library of Congress Control Number: 2009943946

Designed by RoS
Cover design by Garland Kirkpatrick / www.helveticajones.com
Type set in BellCent BdList BT/Myriad Pro

ISBN: 978-0-7643-3437-5
Printed in China

Dedication

This book is dedicated to my wife, Renate, my most enthusiastic supporter and fiercest critic, without whom none of this would have been possible.

Acknowledgements

This book would not have been possible without the unfettered access provided by Jesse Hernandez, owner of the School of Hard Knocks and Empire Wrestling Federation in San Bernardino, California. As a trainer and promoter, Jesse is the backbone of these organizations and the success each wrestler has achieved is due in large part to his mentoring. Thank you, Jesse.

Thank you to the many men and women who allowed me to photograph them, to watch them succeed and fail, moment by moment, as wrestlers. Watching them train in the evenings after a hard day of work for the chance to wrestle in a match has been immensely entertaining and very humbling. Their courage and determination has made each of them superstars. I hope my pictures do justice to their spirit.

Thank you to the many people who supported and encouraged me to continue this project and who provided insight into the pictures over the years. Though I am sure to forget some who made important contributions, they include Susan Joyce, Habib Kheradyar Zamani, Jack Butler, Blake Fitch, Paula Tognarelli, Garland Kirkpatrick, Andi Campognone, Doug McCulloh, Rebecca Trawick, Rick Peres, Stephen Cohen, Tyler Stallings, Karen Sinsheimer, Charles Linder, Mery Lynn McCorkle, Tim B. Wride, Peter Hay Halpert, Don Woodford, Louis Fox, Don Solarzano, John Fleeman, Vince Cianni, David Fahey, Mary Virginia Swanson, Kristina Loughery, Patrick DelliBovi, and all my friends at Freestyle Photographic Supplies.

Thank you to the Office of Academic Research at California State University, San Bernardino, for its generous support of this project over the years.

FOREWORD

Whenever Dick Lane bellowed his signature, "Whoa, Nellie!!" roar of approval, we knew—me, my brothers, and the guys in our neighborhood, that is—that we had just witnessed a marvel. Not that we needed much prompting, however, for even on a black-and-white television in the early-1960s the slaps of flesh against flesh, the sounds of forceful exhalations and unstoppable grunts, and the sights of half-naked bodies careening against taut ropes and slamming against a padded mat brought shouts of acclaim, groans of empathetic torture, and the inevitable squeals of delight and raucous laughter.

Lane was the voice of the Olympic Auditorium in Los Angeles and provided the exhilarated commentary for what were, for us, the most death-defying and accomplished wrestling matches held anywhere in the world. We thrilled when Bobo Brazil and The Sheik squared off for what Lane promised would be the match that would end all matches. We felt personally vindicated when Freddy Blassie (who reminded us all of the mean old guy who lived on the corner and used to turn his sprinklers on us whenever we would get close to walking on his lawn) would be pummeled into smarmy, pleading submission by anyone. And we were puzzled over the circuitous transformations of Hulk Hogan from good guy to bad and back again that surely signaled some deep personality disorder.

That we all survived to recount our experiences is in itself somewhat remarkable, for watching the matches themselves quickly devolved into re-creating them as soon as Lane concluded the post-match interviews with our favorite combatants. Retiring to small patches of lawn—or deep shag carpeting if our mothers were not home—we would inflict the moves and as much harm as possible, short of anything that would cause the inflictee to scurry home crying or bloodied, and hence put an end to the re-creation. We instinctively knew that slamming someone's head against a tree trunk or bashing a chair across an opponent's back would be going too far (Dad would be angry if the tree were harmed and Mom if the chair were scratched), but anything else was seemingly fair game. We tried the claw, figure four leg lock, elbow drops, and wrist locks without seriously maiming one another because when all was said and done, and because we had no size or age classifications, the oldest, the biggest, or the fattest usually won the match by sheer virtue of gravity.

Looking at Tom McGovern's project Hard Boys + Bad Girls brings back these personal memories. More importantly, however, as we as a culture work through the re-thinking necessary in a down-turned economy, the images have much to teach us about dreams, invention, and determination.

To approach these photographs it is necessary to remember that before the Las Vegas theatrics of World Wrestling Entertainment (WWE), there was a low-tech professional wrestling infrastructure that was based less on glamour than grit, less on camera angles than counter-moves, and less on paychecks than perseverance. It is also important to know that this infrastructure still exists today and serves as a feeder circuit, a bridge that spans the chasm between Tuesday night matches in the Knights of Columbus Hall in San Bernardino and WWE's Friday night SmackDown at Staples Center in downtown Los Angeles.

McGovern stakes his position not as a debunker nor as a critic, nor a cynic. His mission is not to reveal a sense of hopelessness, for the dreams and aspirations of his wrestlers command his respect. McGovern does not forefront a tawdry futility, but expresses the genuine expressions of his subjects' talent, skills, and dreams that are only visible in the egalitarian environment of the squared ring. His characterizations are the embodiments of dreams pursued, aspirations to celebrity, and the shimmering specter of success.

McGovern presents us with a balanced view into the alternative, personality-driven world of wrestling that conjoins theatre and athletics. He is enthralled by the environment and characters of small-time wrestling, where the slippage between his subjects' street and arena personas are congruent to the ring's duality as both stage and gym. Yet, McGovern introduces one nore element of slippage that provides his viewers with he merest of cracks through which to supercede the acades, access the aspirations, and inspire empathy or his subjects. How else to explain the portraits of Masked Gringo and Anarchist in their make-shift dress-ng room—their ring-intensity stunningly missing as hey struggle to be anything but two awkward teens. Abraded skin, bruises, and acne testify more to Loki's letermination than does his defiant stance. And the weet, slightly pudgy, and yet somehow unpredictably ootent Sexy Starrlit strikes a pose that seems to convey in assurance that may not exist anywhere else in her life. McGovern allows his subjects' bravado and bluster to nanifest at whatever level they feel most comfortable. He plays the admiring yet relentless audience, seeing nore than most and requiring that the objects of his crutiny play their personas to their logical conclusion: uthenticity.

McGovern's pictorial strategies are not ethnographic ior do they succumb to the current rage for subculture ourism. They are not contingent on a typological study ior do they pay homage to the collection of a set of Arbus-like oddities. He has not lounged in the visual loldrums of colorful costumes nor leached any trace of haracter from his subjects in a sterile search for form. McGovern's is a humanistic undertaking—and, as such, s consistent with his previous bodies of work. He is a eeker in the best sense of the word, questing for what ie can learn, what he can know, and what he can feel by being a part of a world hitherto unknown.

I began by looking through the somewhat nostal-ic haze of pre-adolescent memories. It seems only itting that I should close by retreating back to that ame terrain: to grass-stained knees, jammed fingers, ipped t-shirts, scraped elbows, sweaty hair, and the nowledge that though your head only missed the netal sprinkler-head by an inch, it might as well have been a mile. Most of all, however, it is the recollection of hearing the three-count of a pin—and not being on he bottom. Like McGovern's Hard Boys + Bad Girls, it is he sweet memory of winning.

Tim B. Wride
July, 2009

Tim B. Wride is the Executive Director of the No trings Foundation and the former curator of photo-raphs at the Los Angeles County Museum of Art.

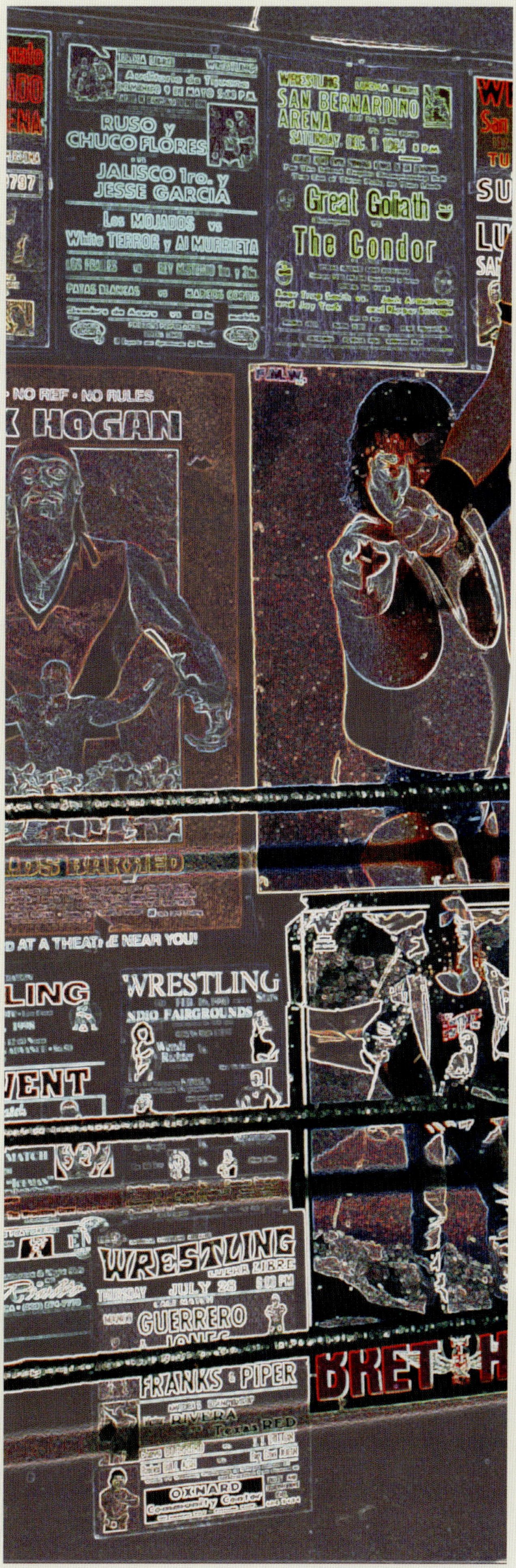

INTRODUCTION

One day while riding my bike a few blocks from home, I came across a storefront with a sign that said, "School of Hard Knocks, Professional Wrestling Training". Like many shops in San Bernardino, the crude hand-painted sign was badly faded and suggested a long-since defunct operation. But then I heard loud thuds coming from inside. I went around to the back of the building and entered. There I found a dozen or so young men and women squeezed into a dank, tiny storefront gym with just enough room for a full-size wrestling ring. I introduced myself to owner and former professional wrestler, Jesse Hernandez, who enthusiastically welcomed me to take pictures. He immediately introduced me to one of his star wrestlers, Johnny Dynamite—both of them seemed a bit disappointed that I didn't have my camera with me right then. I agreed to come back the following day. Thus this project began.

I knew nothing about wrestling other than having watched it on TV a few dozen times in the 1980s, so I had no idea what to expect. I was quickly impressed when I found out how much work it took to be a wrestler, how much thought went into each persona, and how protective they were of each other's well being. On that first day, I remember the trainer calling out, "Watch your partner's head!" as he demonstrated how to cup an opponent's head and neck when slamming them down onto the mat.

This funky little wrestling school is so much more than just a small storefront with a ring, it's the beginning of the pursuit of a dream. The young men and women I met, some on their first day of practice, told me that they have been watching wrestling on TV for as long as they could remember, and it was the only thing they've ever really wanted to do. Very few of these enthusiasts were in school and all had day jobs as truck drivers, warehouse workers, short-order cooks, and cashiers. All carried the improbable fantasy of becoming a famous wrestler. Indeed, if there is one continuous thread to what I witnessed and heard from these wrestlers it is that they were on a quest to realize their dreams of success.

The pursuit of these dreams is manifest in myriac ways: in the hard work it takes to manage a day job and practice four days a week at the wrestling school in the carefully constructed identity, or "gimmick", tha combines comic book characterizations of violence anc sexuality with the deeper realization that each match is an ongoing narrative that pits good against evil; anc in the optimism that allows each wrestler to re-inven themselves with gusto to create a convincing charac ter and story every time they enter the ring—even i its only for a few dozen people watching a match in a parking lot.

But wrestlers can not rely solely on their gimmic to carry them through a match. Wrestlers develop a se of moves that they know by heart. Practice consists o them lining up in the ring to do warm-up exercises one by one—tumbles that bring them back to their feet, firs on the left shoulder, then on the right. Eventually, th trainer stands in the middle of the ring and command the action.

They continue with very basic holds and throws anc then introduce more intricate moves, throwing an op ponent against the ropes followed by a clothesline— forearm to the chest that sends a wrestler to the ma with a loud thud. The scene suggests a ballet, a "mal ballet with blood", according to wrestler Bo Cooper, anc reminds me of Edgar Degas' painting *Monsieur Perrot Dance Class* (c.1875), in which young dancers are line up around the room with the master in the middle, tap ping his walking stick. Similarly, trainer Jesse Hernande barks orders and dispenses praise and criticism as th young wrestlers line up and take turns doing thei shoulder rolls and practicing their falls.

There is something deeply wholesome about thi discipline and dedication. The city of San Bernardin is a blue-collar community that has been down on it luck for a long time. It's a place where the lure of gang and drugs is real and where violence is not somethin you just watch on TV. For these young people, pursuin vrestling takes dedication, focus, and a sense of purpose hat is refreshing.

They give themselves over to the promoter, who elps them come up with a professional persona, which ; at the core of their passion for wrestling. I witnessed his throughout the project as I shared my photographs vith the wrestlers. These young men and women have n inherent understanding that photographs construct n identity, especially a media identity, that is so much nore powerful than who they really are. Amazingly, o one ever blamed me for a bad picture. Instead they velcomed my photographs enthusiastically, scrutinizing ach image for how convincing their persona was. They ook an unconvincing pose or a break in their character s self-criticism and evidence that they must strive to o better.

They understand that photography blurs fiction into act and they consciously use this to re-invent themelves as wrestling superstars. Having grown up with ITV, tabloid journalism, and a 24-hour news cycle, the ubjects were willing to collaborate with me on these onscious constructions of their media personas. They re performance artists who preen and strike poses or the camera—mocking famous TV wrestlers while imultaneously admiring them—all for the magic of eing captured in the pain and glory of their chosen lter egos.

I love that their professional characters can be very illy and juvenile as well as menacing and truly scary. The rst time I met Brawlin' Bo Cooper, a huge young man vith a baby face and killer's stare, he definitely frightned me and I kept my distance. Paranoia is a scrawny id in Gothic attire, all teenage ennui and anger. Ragin' awg wears a dog collar and comes out like an escaped nimal, growling and foaming at the mouth. Bible asher (who really is a preacher) wears a large cross on is chest and hits his opponents with an oversized bible. ino Gambino is a "regular guy" who gets picked on a lot, ut when he puts his beanie on he becomes powerful. esire, who flaunts a dangerous, aggressive sexuality, ums up the wrestler's quest—the desire for fame and uccess, the desire to win, and the manipulation of exual desires to advance an agenda. These names and he images they conjure up are powerful signifiers of ur time and of the subjects' keen understanding, both onscious and subliminal, of what attracts people to vrestling and what keeps them coming back. It's also interesting to note that if the fans don't respond to a character, the wrestler will dump it and come up with a new one. It all gets back to entertaining the audience and telling a story through the action in the ring.

Wrestling is a larger-than-life manifestation of the zeitgeist that un-scripted television programming has tapped into. It is the crazy dream lived, the thrill of real and imagined violence, and the comedy of outrageous parody combined with physical pain and the threat of public humiliation. There is also the thrill of the live match in a small high school gym or Knights of Columbus hall and watching the battle royale happen in real time before your eyes. For all its largess, this is a quaint practice that reminds me of the zealous performers and mesmerized fans of a traveling circus or tent revival. Some of this is due to the fact that in a small venue it's a lot harder to fake a punch when fans are only ten feet away. Despite stomping on the mat to accentuate the experience of delivering a blow, it still must hit its mark and the bright red handprint on a wrestler's skin attests to its authenticity.

There is a strong sexual undercurrent throughout wrestling that is less homosexual than erotic. It is more a reflection of our sexualized culture where stimulation is used as a marketing lure. The clash of body against body, the grabbing hands, and agonizing facial expressions are easily seen as ecstatic. The women wrestlers flaunt their breasts and openly try to seduce the audience and other wrestlers, hoping to entice their devotion or to disarm their opponents during combat. The muscular, bare-chested men, writhe against each other in an orgasm of sweaty confrontation.

Though professional wrestling has been criticized as a fraud, it has been on the forefront of cultural fascination by blurring fiction into fact. In truth, since it takes a great deal of athleticism to wrestle well, it is very difficult to choreograph and still appear real. Wrestling is different precisely because the outlandish characters are conduits for real physical conflict that is dangerous and even deadly. Professionals who have died in the ring have proven this point. The young men and women of the School of Hard Knocks experienced tragedy in June 2004, when a 19-year-old novice died three days after suffering a head injury during practice.

Wrestling and its outrageous characters and good versus evil story lines appeal to blue-collar America, where learning a trade or enlisting in the military is often more accessible than a college degree or white-collar career. That these young people find inspiration from something that is so difficult to perform, and that they pursue a dream that is so unlikely, is deeply moving. Dreams are what keep us going—the dream of getting rich and famous, of marrying a beautiful or handsome spouse, of having a powerful career that demands respect, wearing fashionable clothes, and owning a great car. Like the kids shooting hoops at midnight, dreams are what keep these wrestlers focused, and their hunger for success is what drives them.

Professional wrestling is a quintessentially American invention that combines aspects of sport, drama, and entertainment into one wildly eclectic package. As a sport it is truly athletic and rigorous. I have watched these young men and women push their bodies and minds to their physical limits, suffering injury or worse—humiliation.

Closely examine these pictures and you will see a level of determination that belies the loosely coordinated and rehearsed moves. Blood running down a person's head is real and cuts, bruises, sprains, and torn ligaments are real too. Like all great theater and art, wrestling strives for an authoritative presence, one that transcends the moment and appeals to our fantasies and imagination. Professional wrestling is an apt metaphor for our time and one thing is certain; each fighter may know how the match will end, but no one knows exactly what will happen until then.

When you look at these pictures I hope you will see beneath the surface of the subjects' bravado and notice the slight and vulnerable young person trying desperately to find his or her way in a world where image rules.

Thomas McGovern

THE

Photographs

Melina making an entrance, 2001.

The Masked Gringo and The Anarchist before a match, 2001.

asics
GEL

Sexy Starrlit choking Hurricane Havana, 2005.

Liger Rivera at the School of Hard Knocks, 2001.

Joey Ryan, 2002.

Handsome Johnny Starr making an entrance, 2004.

Yyan Nakano, 2009.

Under Pressure subduing his opponent, 2001.

Jay Blackstar, 2009

Alex Pinchek flying toward Bino Gambino, 2004.

D-Rail diving into his opponents, 2003

Paranoia at the School of Hard Knocks, 2003.

Bino Gambino grabbing the rope, 2004.

Paranoia being helped from the ring, 2002.

The Plague, 2005.

Bino Gambino at the School of Hard Knocks, 2003.

Under Pressure stomping on Sebastian, 2002.

Threat, Desire, and Brawlin' Bo Cooper, 2001.

Steve Masters and his number one fan, 2003.

Hurricane Havana torturing Sexy Starrlit, 2004.

Iceman John Black subduing Johnny Dynamite, 2002.

DK Murphy, 2009.

Steve Masters body slamming Ragin' Dawg, 2003.

Referee, 2003.

Paranoia, 2002.

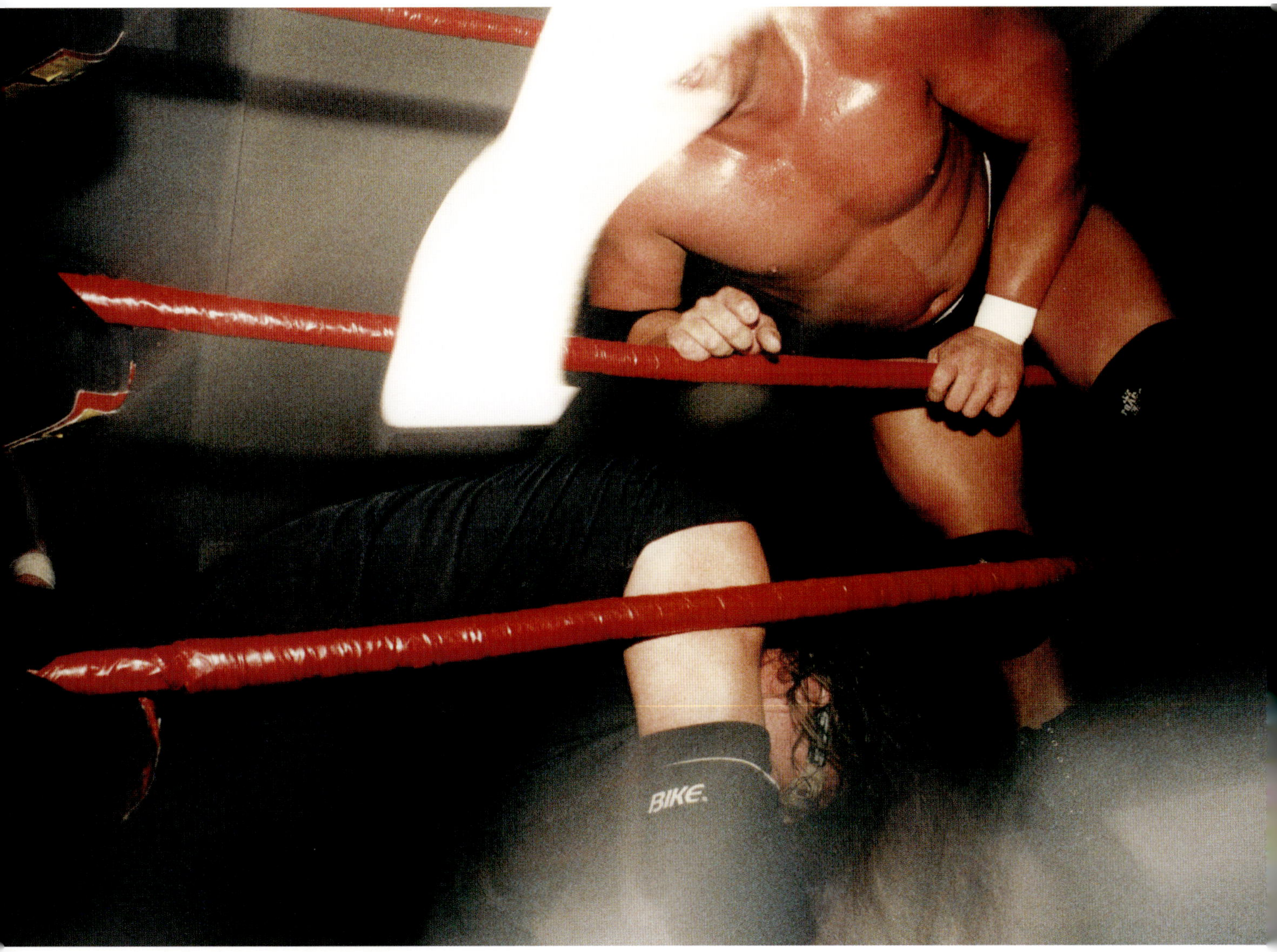

Steve Masters going through the ropes, 2004.

Adam Hoffman, 2009.

Ragin' Dawg making an entrance, 2001.

Steve Masters, Master of Pain, making an entrance, 2003.

The Friar, 2009.

Brawlin' Bo Cooper choking Vizzion, 2002.

Bino Gambino in pain, 2003.

D-Rail, 2001.

Hurricane Havana making an entrance, 2004.

Ghetto Psycho Big Q biting the rope, 2005

Sexy Starrlit after a match, 2004.

Desire attacking Crazy K.C., 2003.

Desire, Jason King, and unidentified wrestler, 2002.

Brawlin' Bo Cooper challenging a fan wearing a Ragin' Dawg t-shirt, 2003.

Omar “Slam” Duncan, 2009.

Desire trying to escape from Melina, 2001.

Robbie Rampage and The Big Kahuna, 2001.

Boys grabbing boys, 2003.

Threat lecturing the fans, 2001.

Under Pressure and Hurricane Marquez, 2002.

Melina, aka Kyra, 2002.

D-Rail and Ragin' Dawg in defeat, 2003.

Harley Wonderland, 2009.

Johnny Dynamite greeting the fans, 2002.

Sergeant Sanders, 2009.

Confrontation outside the ring, 2003.

Johnny Dynamite in agony, 2002.

Rudy Luna with the championship belt, 2003.

Threat pounding Eric Matlock, 2002.

Threat, 2001.

Vizzion thrown into the fans, 2003.

Mighty Mike Mountain, 2009.

Joey Ryan victorious over Vizzion, 2002.

Author's note: These interviews were done some years ago and so they may be outdated or no longer represent the subjects. The ages listed were accurate at the time of the interview. The interviews were transcribed from phone conversations and have been edited for clarity, but always with the intention of accurately representing what was said at the time.

THE

INTERVIEWS

Bino Gambino

DANYL GREENBERG, AGE 18.

I was always athletic, but also creative and I just loved to imagine stuff. I was never really very good at regular sports, like football, and I wasn't good at drawing or singing or any of that. But I've always loved wrestling. I love the adrenaline rush and it was always a dream to be a wrestler and now it's a dream come true. I love everything about it—I love the entertainment aspect, how you can do anything and everything and it's all part of the act and it gets across to a fan that way. It is really interesting to me.

As my character, Bino Gambino, I'm just a normal guy who people mess around with and beat up, but when I put the beanie on I have much more power.

I just graduated from Santa Monica High School and I've been wrestling for about nine months now. My friends are pretty cool with it, but I wish they would like wrestling more, so they'd come out and see me, but they don't really have much interest in it. My mom's very creative but doesn't understand it. All she wishes for is that I don't get hurt. My dad thinks wrestling is full of shit, that it's a stupid thing to do, that you don't really get anywhere from it. But the times he has seen me in the ring he's been pretty happy.

I love working with Jesse because he pushes me really hard. I feel like an ass sometimes because they stop the class to provide special attention for me, but I'd rather they be on me than just saying, "That was ok." My relationship with the other wrestlers is pretty awesome. I've felt very comfortable since the first day I arrived. I really like starting at the bottom and working my way to the top.

Right now, I'm just trying to gain a reputation of deserving to go in the ring and give the show a shot, of deserving to be put on the card. I'm not really working the gimmick, the beanie thing, I'm just trying to get through the show, to be a good wrestler and entertain the fans.

The thing I love about being around wrestlers is that people who get into it are real characters, they have personality. It's cool to meet people with charisma that are unique and that are different. My goal is to be at the top and how long that will take me I don't know. The top would be, of course, to headline WrestleMania, but I feel like I have to be a little more realistic. Maybe just having somebody remember me would be enough, have somebody say, "Remember Bino Gambino? He was an interesting guy to watch."

Alex Pinchek, The Russian Hooligan

Alex Sherman, age 21.

I came to America when I was ten and started watching professional wrestling and loved how much attention those guys were getting. I loved the crowds and their reaction to every move. I really wanted to do that. My attraction to wrestling boils down to attention. I love the high it brings you when there's a big crowd reacting to whatever you do, to every movement. It's my perfect kind of thing—a fight and the high I get from performing.

Usually I play a bad guy, a bad Russian. I'm here in America to prove to the American people that Russian athletes are the best. Americans are fat and lazy and I'm here to prove that Russians are better athletes.

I get along with pretty much all the wrestlers. I try to work out a lot, keep myself in shape, and I guess it's working out okay. Working out takes a lot of self-discipline and that's my biggest problem.

During the day I'm a telemarketer.

My whole theory is you should do what you love to do. Life's an adventure and you should have a goal in life and go with it and have fun and be smart about it.

Desire

Shelly Martinez, age 21.

Ever since I was a little girl I was a huge fan of wrestling and I always wanted to be one. After high school I went to college for a little bit and realized I didn't want to do that, but I didn't know what to do about it. And that's when I got involved in modeling, figuring it would lead to something. A casting director remembered that I used to talk about being a wrestling geek and cast me in a small role in a wrestling movie. That's when I met my first trainer in San Bernardino. I've been in so many matches that I can't remember.

I know a lot of people say it's about the reaction they get from the crowd, but what intrigues me about wrestling is that its like you're putting on a play for the audience with your body. You know who is the good guy and who is the bad guy and when the good guy is getting beat up you want him to come back. You can tell a story without saying a word, you tell it with your body.

When I first started doing shows I was always the heel or bad guy and because of that every federation I've been in I've turned face to become a good guy. Even though I tried to be bad, everybody liked me, partly because there aren't that many girl wrestlers, and, of course, I have boobs and ass—the boys love that. I'm not stupid; I know sex sells. And I give them what they want. I just work with what I have.

Most of my family supports me but my mom and her boyfriend don't and it's kind of rough because I've wanted this forever. They think I should be going to college and get a normal job and they just don't get that that's not where I'll be happy. I was a hard-core daddy's girl and he always told me that if that's what I wanted to be that's what I'd be. He passed away the year I graduated from high school and I know he'd be proud of me.

This is the high point of my career right now. My dream is right there. I want to be in the WWE and I just had my second audition with them and it looks like this summer I may be going to their school in Kentucky. The hardest thing is money—I got so busy wrestling that I was turning down modeling gigs, which pay way more. You can work real hard and finally make it or you quit because you don't have the heart. That's when people fail at trying to get where they want to be.

Hurricane Havana

Sabrina Turkal, age 33.

I got into wrestling after being contacted by a company that was doing wrestling videos about a year and a half ago. And since I have 14 brothers and we fought all the time, I knew I could do this. My family is very supportive and my 9-year-old son is into it too. The fans are what motivate me. Every time I talk to a fan and they tell me how great I am, it makes me want to do it more. The fans are the most important thing in my life. The one piece of advice I give to anyone who wants to be a wrestler is never let anyone tell you that you can't do something. You can do anything you want in life if you work hard.

Iron Warrior

Tony Gomez, age 37.

I became a wrestler because I enjoyed watching it when I was a little kid. I was a street fighter and came from a real poor family. When I met my wife she encouraged me to do it and helped me out. I came to the US when I was four years old and grew up in National City, California. I initially trained with Rich Frisk, a former NWA wrestler. He taught me all the moves. Eventually, one of my friends brought me to Mexico to learn Lucha Libre style wrestling.

Mexican gladiators wear the mask out of tradition and it means everything in the world to them. There are special tournaments where the loser is unmasked and humiliated. You could come back after losing your mask, but it also might mean the end of your career, so we're very protective of the mask.

I know different styles of wrestling and I've competed in cage fights. I have learned the business and will soon be opening the IWW school of wrestling here in Southern California. I've trained with many, many superstars from professional Lucha Libre. I'm also a chef at Outback Steak House and in my free time I take care of my kids and train three or four days a week, because you have to train and maintain your skills. For training I go all the way to Tijuana. I get booked a lot so I guess I'm a good wrestler.

It can be hard being a wrestler when you have a family—I have three little kids and a wife. I've had offers from federations in the U.S. and Japan that I turned down because I love my family, but I love my sport too and sometimes family can get in the way. But my kids encourage me to keep wrestling.

Sweet Candy

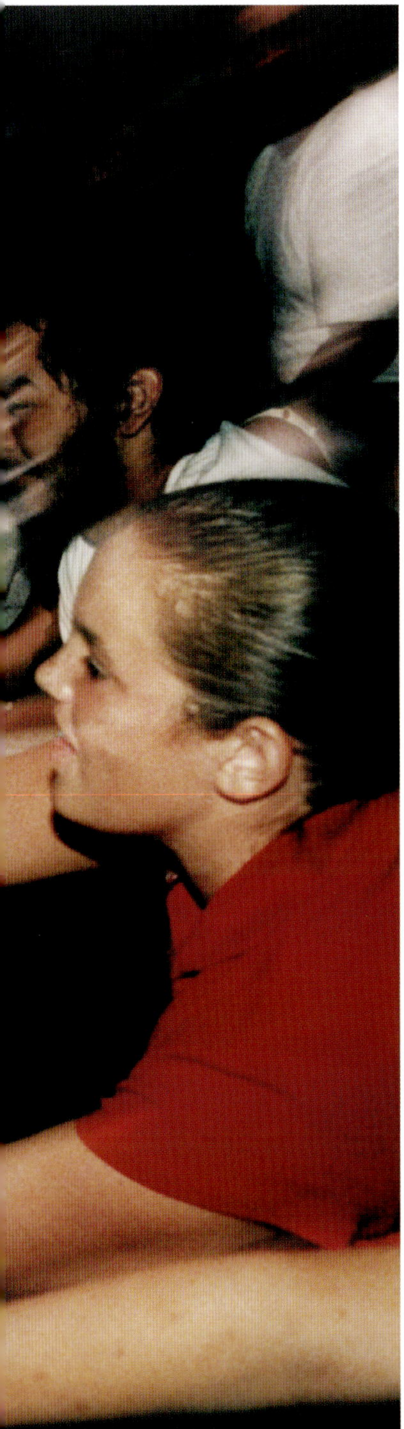

Candice Dawson, age 17.

When I was about six years old I saw Macho Man Randy Savage and ever since then wrestling was all I wanted to do. Even though I'm not big, I have the heart and desire to do it. I have so much desire that I'm not going to let anything get in my way.

Sweet Candy is sweet and energetic and fun loving. I love Shawn Michaels and watch a lot of wrestling on TV. My family pretty much supports it, but they're concerned about me getting hurt. I do a lot of working out on my body and I practice a lot too. I haven't been in many shows yet, but I go to the School of Hard Knocks to train. Sometimes the guys go easy with me, but they get into trouble because they're not supposed to go easy on the girls. For the most part, they treat the women like any of them and they're all pretty cool. I like working with the guys because then I have to be as good as them. It's a challenge kind of thing. There's respect. I'm hoping to make it to the WWE, but if I don't I want to go as far as I can because I want to wrestle for the rest of my life if I can.

Chuck "The Dragon" Lee

Charles Ray Polk III, age 16.

So far I've wrestled two matches with the EWF. My family used to watch wrestling on TV when I was younger and then I had a girlfriend who liked it. Ever since then I have wanted to be a pro wrestler.

I don't really see it as being about the size of your body, I see it as what's in your heart. That comes out in everybody's match. Other guys are bigger but I'm still growing— I'll be there someday. Right now I just concentrate on my skills, my heart, and working the fans.

Over the next few years I'll be wrestling and working and trying to go to junior college. A lot of my friends really look up to me, they're amazed because when we were younger we did backyard wrestling and now I'm in front of the fans.

My family is supportive but my dad and I never had a very strong relationship. But he drives me to the school and matches. He thinks it's all fake and doesn't really like it too much, but he's still supportive of me doing it.

Steve Masters, Master of Pain

STEVE VINEYARD, AGE 32.

Wrestling kinda gets in your blood. I played sports ever since I was a kid, baseball and football. I was a high school and college All American and tried out for the Buffalo Bills. I've been a wrassling fan since I was nine or ten years old and it's the adrenaline of wrestling that I love. A lot of people think it's an individual sport, but it's a team effort. It takes two in the ring to create a show and I've always been a team-oriented person. I learned early on that you're only as good as your opponent.

I can pull a crowd in with the American dream, being the common man, a country boy, and a bad guy—looking tough. I have to thank my parents for some of that!

I'm fortunate that Jesse lets me be a head trainer here. Even though I'm 32 and an old man to a lot of the kids, it takes a lot of maturity to succeed and it puts me in a leadership role. Most kids don't have a lot of maturity in life. A 25-year-old is more like an 18-year-old twenty years ago and that affects performance in the ring.

You can make it with heart in wrestling, where you can't in other sports. Others are based on performance, not entertainment. The wrestling business is the most physical sport I've been in, but there's certainly a lot more to it than just going out there and hitting someone.

Rudy Luna

Rudolfo Arillano, age 27.

I've been wrestling for 13 years, since I was 14. My dad's a wrestler (Big Rudy). He was training with a bunch of guys out of San Bernardino at the time. I had seen him on TV and I wanted to give it a shot, too. My dad is obviously very supportive but my mom doesn't like it very much. I had some family problems because she didn't want me to do it. By the second practice she accepted the fact that I was going to, but then I came home with a fractured eye socket and she had that "Oh, shit!" look on her face. Over the years I've had several different gimmicks, but right now I'm half of the tag team West Coast Ryders.

Wrestling encompasses so many different things, one is the athletic part, which I love. Another is the entertainment part. Having kids come up to you is great, but it takes a lot of effort to find the right combination of physicality and entertainment to make the crowd go, "Ooh" and "Aah". Show them something they've never seen, like you've gotten beat up and you still walk away, and they say, "That looks good!"

My relationship with the fans is good. A lot of the Hispanic fans are really supportive which surprised me since I'm kind of a bad guy. After the matches I'm signing autographs and folks ask me how they can get started. There is such a love in it all that you can't quit, it becomes part of your life. You try to walk away because of injuries, but you have to come back. I think that has something to do with the friends and camaraderie, everyone helping each other out. It's almost like an extension of your family. When I go to shows I see guys and shake their hands and even give them hugs. I don't hug most of my family, but I do with these guys because I put my life in their hands and theirs in mine, and there is so much trust.

A lot of people don't realize that once you step foot in the ring you have the possibility of not walking out. You have to do your best or you can get really hurt. As Jimmy Superfly Snuka said, "If you got hurt, you should have been in the gym more."

Of course, everyone looks for that contract with the WWE, but most of the time it doesn't happen. You gotta be content with what you're doing, with where you're at right now. I'm content with where I'm at, but I always want to take that next step, one more step up on the ladder because I have a bad fear of failing. I am so scared of failing. That's what drives me the most, the fear of failing. That whole purpose of not failing has helped keep me out of trouble! I looked inside myself and said I don't want to fail at this, keep going and keep trying harder. It's a one in a million shot but if I get that shot I want to know that I gave it my all. I don't have to make it, just get that shot.

Handsome Johnny Starr

John Akes, age 21.

Since I was a kid I've watched pro wrestling with my dad. I love watching old wrestling, too, from the 60s to 80s. In the 80s, the fans believed everything they did. When I was twelve we saw WrestleMania 12, when Shawn Michaels beat Bret Hart and won the championship belt. From then I knew that that was what I wanted to do. My family has come to numerous shows and they're very supportive. They were there for my debut match and the night I won the belt.

I started training in 1999 when I was fifteen and during the day I work in my family's funeral home business.

When I first started I wish I had taken this advice: get to a gym, work out and build you body to where you actually look like a professional wrestler, so when you walk through the curtain, a fan will take you seriously. Stick to it and don't give up.

When I first got into the wrestling business I didn't care so much for the fans, but now my attitude has changed. I love that I can go out there and be myself or be somebody else, I can entertain and I can capture the fans attention and hold on to it for the time I'm out there. I'm a ham and I enjoy going out there and being goofy. My persona is what I really want to be. I want to be the sexy boy, the man every woman wants to be with. And what guy doesn't want that?

I personally don't see two guys in tights beating each other as being at all sexual. But some people are freaks and that's what they like. I've done a gay gimmick. I wore a mask, Speedo, pink thong, and a pink and green sports bra, and gave the biggest, meanest looking guy in the crowd a lap dance. It wasn't sexual, it was comedy, it was fun.

The whole reason a person is in professional wrestling is to be the top dog in the business. In ten years I want to be on my way to being a future legend. I want to wrestle at WrestleMania in the main event for the world title.

Johnny Dynamite

JAN ERIC OHRSTROM, AGE 21.

I've been wrestling almost six years now. It's been my dream to do this since I was four. I remember this vividly—my mom was cleaning the house one day and I was annoying her so she put me in front of the TV. The first thing that came on was wrestling. I watched one match and was immediately hooked! It was between The Rockers, Shawn Michaels and Marty Genetti, and Tito Santana and Rick Martel.

I've temporarily paralyzed myself twice and I've taken some pretty nasty falls, but it doesn't even come to mind when my music hits, I'm jumping and pumping myself up, and I hear people screaming for me. And it doesn't matter if there are ten people screaming for me, a thousand, or even eight thousand, like I've seen before. The adrenaline kicks in and it's like living in Nirvana, you're living your dream. When I come out to fight, I look around and know that this is what I was meant to do. A lot of my friends didn't take me seriously at first but now they're real supportive.

I have always thought it kind of funny that girls scream for me because I've never thought of myself as that kind of guy. It is so funny to see girls of all ages yelling and screaming, "Johnny I love you!" and wanting to give me their phone numbers. I actually had a four-year-old come up and ask me to marry her mom.

I've worked odd jobs to support my wrestling—Best Buy, security, whatever. I plan to be wrestling full time in no later than five years and my absolute top goal is to be in the WWE no later than 10 years. I thank God that my mentor is Jesse Hernandez because he's been showing me the right way to do this. Without him I don't think I would have gotten as far as I have. I do feel I will be able to make it. I'm very consistent with physical training and I've changed my diet and focused on my goals. I feel that with Jesse's leadership I'll be able to make an impact.

My parents didn't take me seriously for a long time and thought it was a phase I'd grow out of. But once I started making it big, going to a lot of places and traveling with the top leagues in Mexico, getting booked on really big shows, they started to get proud of me and tell their friends.

Vizzion

ADAM HARBOUR, AGE 29.

I've been a wrestling fan since about 1985 and grew up watching Hulk Hogan and Macho Man Randy Savage. I fell in love with the sport and never lost the desire to do it. I thought I could be a wrestler because my heart was in it. I'm a pretty religious guy and the Lord has never taken it out of my heart. My belief has everything to do with how I wrestle—before a match I get on my knees and ask the Lord to be with me in the ring, to protect me as well as my opponent. It's by HIS strength that I have strength.

My career is going great. I'm getting known and even had someone come to my job that recognized me—that was so neat! I'm having a blast, I couldn't ask for anything better. During the day I sell concrete accessories to the construction industry.

My family is very supportive and they don't miss a show. I told my dad a long time ago I wanted to be a wrestler and he thought it was the dumbest thing he ever heard, but now he's my biggest fan. He thought it was just a childhood dream. He wanted to be a pro baseball player when he was younger, but has been working at the same job for 35 years now, so you can imagine his dismay when I said I wanted to be a wrestler. He envisioned me staying in school and going to college.

Vizzion is basically me with a twist. My vision has always been my Achilles heel. It's been bad ever since I can remember and I have a degenerative condition in my right eye, so my vision is 20/400—that's why I wear the goggles.

My character is the ultimate good guy and I also sport a mullet hair cut—business in the front and party in the back. People just want to love the mullet. I don't quite understand it, but people dig it!

Sexy Starrlit

Shelly Turner, age 18.

I've been wrestling for about six months. I had been watching my boyfriend Patrick for a while and just wanted to try it. I make sandwiches at Hogi Yogi during the day.

My grandparents don't like it too much—wrestling with guys and training with them, but they're okay that I do it. My friends aren't into it either. My cousin used to watch it on TV and I wasn't too into it then, but I'm getting more into it now. I just try to train the best I can, not be too girly-girly about it. I'll see where it takes me; I just do it for fun now.

I'm planning on going to Riverside Community College next year for cosmetology and keep wrestling too. My advice to other women who want to wrestle is be careful, you can get hurt real bad, so take it seriously.

The fans and I don't get along too well. Sexy Starrlit is cocky and thinks she's too good for everybody. I like that relationship a lot because it gets me hyped and makes me more energetic. It makes me want to keep wrestling.

Ghetto Psycho Big Q

Quenzell Swayne, age 30.

I've been wrestling ten years and met Jesse Hernandez in Las Vegas. When he'd do a show, Jesse would call and say (you gotta imitate his voice when you say this): "Brother, get your black ass down here!" I've trained with a lot of the old school guys, but Jesse's the main trainer I've worked with. Outside of wrestling I've been a bouncer for 12 years for some pretty rough clubs where every weekend we'd have shootouts and I'd be dodging bullets.

The wrestling business got into my blood when I was about 15. I started play wrestling with my friends. The motivation to drive from Las Vegas to Los Angeles just to be in a match, for me, is to make it to the big time. It keeps me out of trouble.

My family loves me being a wrestler. My grandmother came to a show when I was wrestling with Ice Man John Black. We were tag team partners called The West Side Niggas. She was very happy to see me wrestle before she died in 2002. That meant a lot to me.

My character comes from my life experiences growing up in South Central Los Angeles, hanging out with the wrong element and living the gang lifestyle. I was a big kid and a lot of folks were recruiting me. The ghetto life is all I knew and it shaped me.

I love making people laugh. Where else can you act the clown? I do my best to make stuff happen when I'm wrestling. I'm gonna give it about ten more years and if something big doesn't happen, then I'm done. My advice to young wrestlers is to get a good education first, then wrestle. Don't let it be your only livelihood, have something else to fall back on. Keep close to your family and keep yourself humble. Listen first, then be heard.

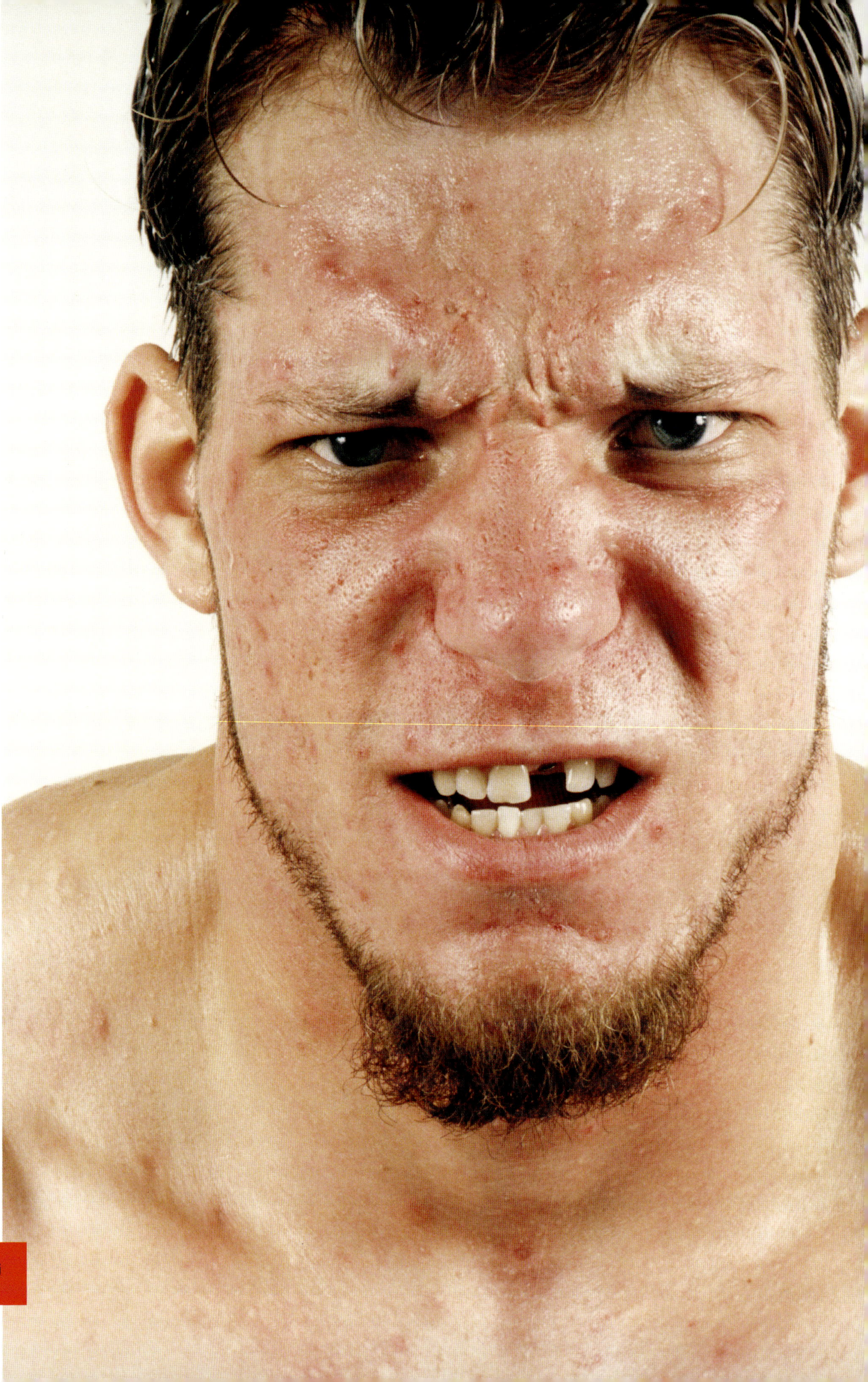

Loki

Pete Thomas Schaffer, age 23.

I haven't wrestled in a long time. I only did it for fun. I always enjoyed watching it since I was a kid and a friend of mine, The Suicide Kid, wrestled with Jesse and that's how I got hooked up. I just did it for fun, messing around, getting a good workout. I really enjoyed it though. It's one of the more physical sports—you get real winded and sore.

I'm getting ready to start up as a mental health worker through training I received in the Army Reserves. Another thing I've done since I was a kid was play video games so another career option I'm considering is going back to school for computer programming to design video games.

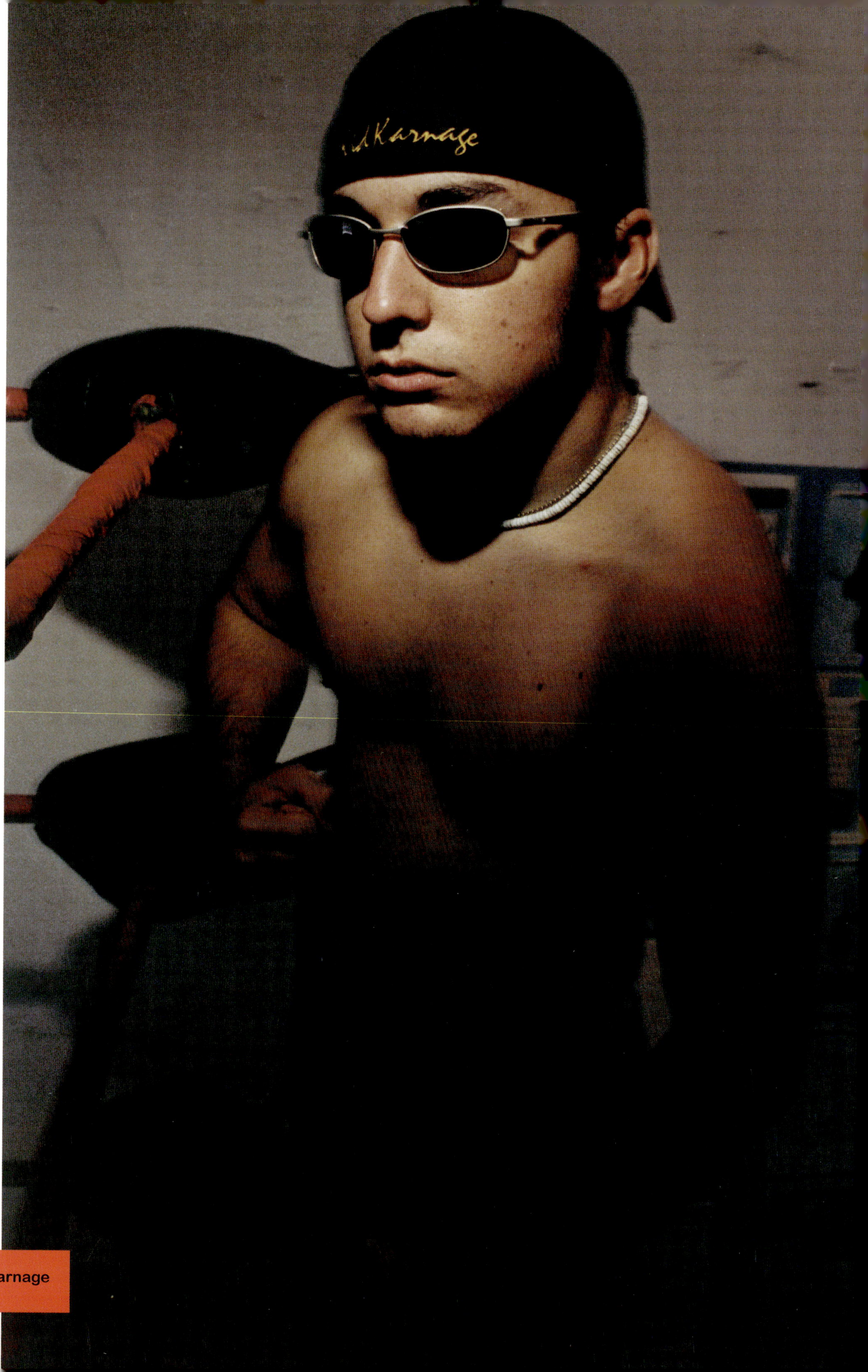

Kid Karnage

Tyler Davidson, age 16.

I've been wrestling professionally with Jesse for about three years now, since I was 13 years old. I showed up at the school in December 1999 and have been going ever since. At first my parents were a little apprehensive because they didn't know about the safety issues, but now that I've been doing it for a while, they love it. I just got my learner's permit, so hopefully once I start driving you'll be seeing me in more shows.

We've gotten to the point now where most people know wrestling is entertainment, but an important aspect of getting into it is the suspension of disbelief, really letting yourself go and letting yourself believe in what's happening. A lot more people understand that it isn't fake as much as it is show business. I'll tell you, get into the ring and take bumps for an hour and you'll know for sure that it ain't fake! You really want to push a wrestler's buttons? Call him a phony! Guys got the scars and injuries to prove it isn't fake.

The original idea for the Kid Karnage gimmick was a real dark character—not so much evil as a brooding teenager with angst. It sort of modifies depending on whom I'm wrestling. Most of the time I'm wrestling a guy much bigger than me so I play the underdog in the match.

I'm not sure where I'll be in a few years, but hopefully a bit higher up, bigger promotions and matches. I'm still young, so I have time to grow. I'll stay in school though. I'm looking for a job, but right now I work for my father who sells heavy equipment like bulldozers. I answer the phones for him and I go to Riverside Poly High. I love English and foreign languages and want to study journalism and continue writing poetry. I have written about wrestling once or twice, but the poetry I write isn't good unless it's on something dark. I find myself writing as Kid Karnage.

My Life

I stand behind the curtain, ready to walk
As I hear the crowd murmur and talk.
They announce my name, my music plays
As my real personality slowly fades.
The transformation is complete,
I'm not the same anymore,
I'm my alter-ego, yelling, screaming,
Looking to settle the score.

You may call this fake or phony if you will,
You tell me it's not a career, it can't pay the bills.
But this is more than that, this is more than it seems
It's my life, my hope, my aspirations, my dreams.

My boots make a dull thud as they hit the hard floor
I scream at the fans, they just yell for more.
You tell me to be normal, grow up, get a life
But guess what, this is what I do, this is my life.

- Kid Karnage

Brawlin' Bo Cooper

ROBERT COOPER, AGE 23.

My gimmick is Brawlin' Bo Copper, a big guy who isn't fraid to take on any opponent. I'm real vicious in the ng and can be a fan favorite or a pretty hateful person. ve been wrestling seven years now. My first match was n May 4, 1996 against Crazy K.C. with the Empire Wresing Federation. My first gimmick was called The Hangnan. The Hangman was an executioner and I would ome out with a noose and all that. That first match was t the old San Bernardino Boys and Girls Club and there vere about 300 people and it was pretty cool.

I've always wanted to wrestle. I was always infatuted with the WWF when I was a kid and my mom used o take me to the shows. When I was about 12 years old he took me to the LA Sports Arena and I walked up to wrestler and asked how I could become one. He told ne that I was too young, but gave me a piece of paper nd said to call when I was a little older. That wrestler vas the late Louie Spicolli. About two years later, when I vas 14, I was listening to Shadow's Wrestling Radio Talk how and he mentioned a school in San Bernardino. So I alled and showed up. I still had that little piece of paper nd one of the promoters recognized the handwriting s Louie's, who had also trained there. About two weeks ater Louie showed up and he remembered me. He kinda ook me under his wing. He played a lot of ribs on me, out he was my biggest inspiration in the business and vhen he passed away I was devastated.

My mom has been my biggest supporter of all. She oaid for my wrestling school and she's always been upportive and always knew that this was my dream. My biggest inspiration, besides Louie and my trainers, s my mom. She made it happen. Sometimes she still drives me to the shows!

When I'm not wrestling I do a lot of bouncing work, out I'm also a telemarketer and I'm engaged. I want to nake the most of my wrestling career, but the business changes every day. I just want to remain active and nake more money than I do now, but I can't predict the uture. Four years from now Vince McMahon's son could oe running the WWE and completely change it—maybe he'll want midget wrestling!

Brawlin' Bo Cooper ragging on an elderly fan, who was a regular at the matches until her death. This picture was on the casket at her funeral.

I was taught by Jesse Hernandez and Bobby Bradley to always be respectful to the fans. If you disrespect a fan when you are out of character, they're not going to want to come back and see you. There was a sweet old lady that I would always heel on and she had the picture of me yelling at her on her casket. She was a very nice lady and I would thank her after the show, when I was out of character.

Jesse is my trainer and taught me pretty much everything I know about the business, he was the one who got in the ring and showed me right from wrong. Bobby Bradley, who works with Jesse, is my best friend in the whole business. He's a tough son of a bitch, but I listen to him because he's right. He's been around so long. Jesse teaches me how to wrestle and Bobby teaches me the psychology.

The psychology of wrestling is how to tell a story in the ring. Anyone who's a trained wrestler can do a bunch of moves, but without telling a story it makes no sense. That's what the psychology of wrestling is. You gotta do the moves at an exact time. You gotta make sure that you tell a story and know the reasons you're doing those certain moves at that time. Anyone can go out and body slam someone, but it has to be at the right time so the crowd can really pop for you. That's how the crowd thinks—you gotta put on a story. It's just like watching a play or a ballet, a male ballet with lots of blood and guts!

Under Pressure (left) with Iceman John Black.

Jason Eric Sanders, age 28.

I've been wrestling since 1998. It was something I wanted to do for a long time. I was in the Navy and had a part time job doing security at a sports arena in San Diego. I used to work the wrestling shows and got to know some of the guys and they got to know me. I was talking to Mankind (Mick Foley) and he knew Bill and Jesse from The School of Hard Knocks. On my 24th birthday I walked into the School of Hard Knocks and started training. I wrestled in high school and junior college and have been watching professional wrestling since I was five years old and you know me, I'm a ham!

For an entire year I studied wrestling, that's all I did. I watched wrestling and actually paid attention to what they were doing. I paid attention to the moves and worked on my character. My wife thought I was crazy—I would stand in front of the mirror and I would talk to myself and now it's finally paid off.

The original Under Pressure character was a street fighter. He was under social and economic pressure and he was angry at the world and that fueled his desire to fight. He got tired of beating people up on the mean streets of San Diego and wanted to take it global and wrestling was the way to do that.

Iceman John Black and myself had a tag team called "Cash Money Brothers". We didn't want to do the typical gangsta thing. We were businessmen and wrestling was our business. We'd go out there dressed sharp as a tack and after I whooped ya, I'd strangle you with my tie. The tie was my prop.

My friends think it's a blast. They come to matches and I have old Navy buddies who keep track of my character by checking it out on the web.

If given the opportunity, the sky's the limit. There are better technical wrestlers than me in Southern California, but honestly, I don't think there's a better entertainer. Every show that I do, whether I'm a good guy or a bad guy, people remember me. I talk to the fans a lot and their participation is very critical to me. I love it when the fans yell at me because I yell right back—I love it!

I appreciate fans that really believe it's real and we definitely have some of them. I've actually had fans want to fight me. We did a show in Lucerne Valley and John Black, Threat, and myself were the only black people in the building and I have never been called nigger so much in my life! Little kids, 5-6 years old, yelling, "You nigger! You nigger! We hate you!" But it was great and Iceman and I played it to the hilt. True feelings were coming out. We were wrestling two white guys and we were beating the crap out of them and the fans couldn't stand it!

Ragin' Dawg

JONATHAN FRANCIS CEDILLO, AGE 28.

I grew up a wrestling fan from as long as I can remember. I was always into it and had it in my head that I was gonna be a wrestler, but never knew how to go about doing it. I used to get picked on in High School because it wasn't cool to be a wrestling fan and I got teased a lot because I used to talk about becoming a wrestler. As a kid I didn't like school and I was constantly in trouble. But I've also been a camera hog and class clown my whole life—I've always been a ham.

At one point I was having a really hard time in my life. I was homeless and living in my car and then my aunt hooked me up with this movie deal to be an extra in Man on the Moon with Jim Carey. They were filming at the Grand Olympic Auditorium in Los Angeles and I was part of the scene where Jerry Lawler supposedly broke Andy Kaufman's neck. I got a chance to meet Jerry Lawler and asked him how to go about becoming a wrestler and he told me about Jesse Hernandez and The School of Hard Knocks in San Bernardino.

There wasn't anything that told me, "You can be a wrestler," other than the fact I wanted it so badly. I think one of the biggest reasons I wanted to do it was because people told me I couldn't, and that's been my method of operation my whole life. I'll go the extra mile just to prove them wrong.

Currently I'm seeking employment. I had a job working at a bowling alley as a short order cook, but I lost that job because I had a booking and my boss wouldn't let me off. I had to choose between the job and my dream. Anybody who ever gets an autograph from me, I always sign it, "Keep raging and always obey your dreams." I'm a father too and I've sacrificed a lot to be a wrestler—it's put my daughter on the backburner. She's really the only person I worry about in regard to my decision to be a wrestler.

Right now my future is kinda cloudy. My dream takes me to working with the McMahon family of the WWE. I'm having to take the long road to get there because I do have a weight problem and they're very cosmetic—you have to have "the look".

A lot of credit goes to Jesse Hernandez for my gimmick. He didn't like my original character, Rage. There was nothing to it and so I was training a lot and wasn't getting booked. I finally got frustrated and went up to Jesse and asked him to tell me what gimmick he wanted me to have. He said I see you as a dog—your mannerisms, the way you act in the ring, you're a dog! Thus Ragin' Dawg was born. I started in Mexico and I'm a champion down there for WWA and I'm just waiting for that recognition to grow.

The School of Hard Knocks and Empire Wrestling Federation

Original home of The School of Hard Knocks, San Bernardino, California, 2002.

Founded by former professional wrestler Jesse Hernandez, The School of Hard Knocks has been in business longer than any other professional wrestling school in California. The school continues to enjoy a professional reputation; many successful wrestlers have started their careers there. No other school in the area can truthfully make that claim.

The affiliated Empire Wrestling Federation is one of the premier organizations for professional wrestling events in Southern California.

If you would like more information about training for a career as a professional wrestler or to find out about upcoming EWF wrestling matches, visit the Empire Wrestling website at www.empirewrestlingfederation.com, or email Jesse Hernandez (wresref@aol.com).

WRESTLING
RECREATION CENTE
JOHNSON CITY
THUR. DEC. 3
RONNIE ETCHIS
PEDRO ZAPATA
WRIGHT
BELKA
STEINER
WALK
LEGENDS
WRESTLING
CITY AUDITORIUM
FRI. MAY 10
Return Championship Match
DICKIE
STEINBORN
VS
TARZAN TYLER
NO TIME LIMI
WRESTLING
ON PAY-
JOHN CENA
SUMME
SLAM
LEGEN
WREST
WRES
SANDCASTLE
BLACKPOOL
TOP U.K. & WORLD STARS
BIG DA
Marty JONES
ALAN KILBY